consumed

consumed
the survivor's story
u n L Y S H e d

consumed: the survivor's story
Text Copyright © 2023 by alyssia unLYSHed mccloud.
All rights reserved. This book or any portion thereof may not be reproduced or used in any manner whatsoever without the express written permission of the publisher except for the use of brief quotations in a book review or critical articles. For information, address publisher by emailing contactlysh@iamunlyshed.com.
ISBN: 979-8-9884352-0-4
Printed in the United States of America First Printing, 2023.
ig: @iamunlyshed

to the eMpire:
you never should have had to carry my hope for living; yet, in my weakest moments, you held that heaviness without struggle or complaint. you have been the embodiment of love, hope, reason and safety. you cradled me in the strength of our bond each time i tried to hide myself from the Son. you shaped me, embraced me, and gave me permission to fly. you are God's—and you are mine, immediately after.
i love you.
i thank you.

to my Shoota:
you are the first soul outside of my blood that saw all the people inside of me and took the time to meet and befriend each one. you are the first soul outside of my blood who never needed a break or a pause or an ending. you are the first soul outside of my blood that loved me Christ-like.
you are seen completely. you are loved irrevocably.
i thank you.

                              …also.

to macey:
> my guardian angel who is flesh and bone and quite
> literally shows me The Way.

and to the victims, and the victims that didn't know they was victims:
> i love you. so does the Son.

table of contents

before you read:

wrath

woe

healing

happy

before you read:
hey you.

there are quite a few references to blood in this book—but the truth is people "get" blood. in my culture, if you fall and bump your head, you might get one response, but the response would be totally different if you bumped your head and there was *blood*. what's shared here is the kind of urgent that is blood flow, and it may be difficult in some places to keep turning the pages. know that i wrote as God led me, and i think from here the tides can change, but i needed to finish this story so that i can begin to learn and enjoy and lead as my freed self; my *unLYSHed* self. if you're here, i believe this experience is for the sake of your unLYSHed-self too, and *i selfishly want you to finish*. i've lived the dangers of staying in wrath and woe too long, so i don't want you to plant yourself there because you couldn't quite see freedom—*this* book will arrive at *happy*. writing this experience was like trying to untangle a spider's web while preserving each thread. the journey to *happy* required a sorting—a confronting. and each part that was knotted was both delicate and necessary. the Giver of Freedom set me on a task. to entice you to reject *your* bondage and acknowledge that suffering is not your resting place; to encourage you on your journey to freedom; to introduce you to or reacquaint you with *Him*—Freedom's Father. when you close this book, i pray you do so handing in your chains to let them rust for the rest of your days. thank you for being here; for holding my second born in your hands, for praying for my exaltation, the same way that i pray for yours. i implore you: read—*listen*—'til you feel inspired to heal. 'til you recognize your happy. 'til you decide for yourself to become **free**.

with all my love—you are *worthy*.

LYSH

like a little girl sitting over a bowl of ice cream
kicking her feet hanging from her kitchen chair
thinking of nothing
expecting even less
i open the Good Book
i bow my head and close my eyes
i finish praying between heartbeats
then go on in my living
like a little girl
sitting over a bowl of ice cream
kicking my feet hanging from my kitchen chair
thinking of nothing
expecting even less
today would be my day of reckoning
i saw my bowl levitate
i heard
a herd
harmonize from inside it
my legs spilled over onto the floor
stretched out into my front yard
and left my body at the kitchen table
i panicked
then looked up
God was sitting on my sofa
when i prayed
i told Him of what i was afraid
i thought the words would sit in the atmosphere
sandwiched between heaven and my mama's roof
God came personally to say to me
that's not how this works
He patted me on my head
and called me by name
o ye of little faith
He placed His finger on my nose
and i drifted into sleep
i awakened
to see my fears
sitting at my kitchen table
eating my ice cream
kicking their legs
and staring back at me
as i stood gawking
they said to me
you're going to want to sit for this

break me:

Take a match—a flimsy piece of wood with a hot head.
Drag it across a rough surface with just the right amount of pressure.
Watch it wake up in flames.
Take me, with a hot head.
A beaten heart.
A frail body.
A flimsy faith.
Grate my face across the rough surface of everything that makes me tremble, stops my breath, feeds my doubt, and starts my tears.
There would be fire.

There *was* fire.

It started at 6am.

The Sunflower Project was a beautiful beginning. I remembered that next to God's surgical tools was the table where I was pinned by the stem. I could still see the operation room clearly in my mind even though I was far removed from that process, and I remembered being distracted by a sound that, in one season, I had loved above all. 6 months ago, *he*—The Only Man I Ever Wanted to Call "*Baby*"—had whispered my name. His voice was laced with just the right amount of lament; it had repented. It declared its desire for me—it dripped with its *need* of me; and I quickly found that it could still coax me right out of my skin. I remembered leaving the table before God completed the work He had begun, interrupting the process to respond to the call of the soul to which I was *bound*; the tie between us decades strong, weighted with chains and obligation. I had no choice—like clockwork, I became a devoted servant who had no other option but to tell God to pause so that I may respond to the lover that I had longed for—The Only Man I Ever Wanted to Call "*Baby*"— the one who had called my name.

That was then.

Then, I kissed him back like I wanted to suck salvation from his tongue. I searched his mouth for sustenance, pressed my body into his with a confidence that in his hands, in his chest, and on his lips was the elixir that would make life without love *worth* it—like my ravenous desire to belong to him had finally met the day it would be satiated. Our soul tie was revived in our mouth-to-mouth, with no objection from me. I let him have *all*—I opened up my body to The Only Man I Ever Wanted to Call "*Baby*," the man I believed was made to see inside to the place where love had refused to dwell, where love should have been but had been beaten back to hope for *him*. I flung open the windows and doorways and showed him the graveyards and stretches of desert, the spirit and the grounds that craved him, while "*finally*" and "*yes*" manifested on my skin. My hands on either side of his face pulled him more deeply into me, and I showed him how his touch raised up what had been buried inside of me—I devoured his lips as my essence gathered and expanded, showing her bruises from being held down and knocked back, and bloomed in my eyes and in his mouth. Tears streamed down my face as she began to speak in what I knew was the language only my forever would understand, and I smiled because I had given "forever" his name.

    I wanted him.
    I loved him.
    I chose him.

    I drew away from his arms that had only held me limply and released his mouth slowly, the last of him for me to let go the tip of his bottom lip gently held within my smile. I opened my eyes as the same mouth that had just stolen my kiss, the same mouth that had claimed to want me and only me, whispered against my trembling chest—

    "*You're too aggressive.*"

    I reined in my intensity as I studied his golden irises for any trace of my soul floating there; I waited for understanding to jolt him and change the scenery and was filled with disappointment when it never came. Even when spoken to *him*—The Only Man I Ever Wanted to Call "*Baby*"—the language of what was resting deep in my spirit would not know resurrection—it never even made it to his ears. He had no idea where he was when he was next to me; he had no idea who he was holding with me sitting in his lap. With only a little of me off the leash, The Only Man I Ever Wanted to Call "*Baby*" had labeled me as "*too*."

    Spiritual.
    Affectionate.
    Intellectual.

Aware.

Alive.

My heart rate slowed, and I tucked away my longing, knowing in the smallest, most honest place inside of me, that he wasn't the *one*—

But he had already touched me.

Already *kissed* me.

In a Judas moment, someone somersaulted out of holding in my chest and stretched to claim my fingertips, my tongue, and everything between my legs. I was ravenous, bloodthirsty, and revitalized as the woman who lived for *him*—the same kind of girl I was in the sowing; a girl who *could not leave him.*

That led me to *burn.*

It was 6am.

My eyes were locked onto the window in the far corner of my bedroom; back and forth I rocked, my knees pressed into my chest, my arms wrapped tightly around my legs as I stared, my only accompaniment the creaking of my rocking chair. There was no room for my old self in my new body, but my new self only knew my old paths. Over that bypass. Down that dirt road. Into his arms—or wherever he asked me to be. My former routes still led to the same destinations:

Loneliness.

Torment.

Shame.

unLYSHed me couldn't take that.

unLYSHed me became consumed.

With fire.

With rage.

I wondered how I would explain the burns to all of my sunflower sisters. I had moved wrong—thought wrong. This would not be a tale of the restorative power of God as I had assumed it would be from the moment he called to me. He and I would not be the evidence of the dead things that God gave life, the abuse that God turned to love, though it could be a story of how new wine can't go in old wine skins, how new wine in old wine skins will rip the old apart, and spill all over everything around, and be without form, and without a safe place to land and to rest, and I couldn't tell them that I was new and didn't know how to be, or where to go, or who would hold me, I couldn't tell those who stood in the sunflower fields with me of how he had promised I could trust him, of how brave I had tried to be, of how I lost control, or maybe never really had control, and how I stood by and did nothing when the suffering started again, or how my blood coveted his body, how I had never been able to deny him, how denying him had always meant punishment later for me, and how I wasn't brave enough to gamble with his presence, how I feared a wrong move on my account could mean loneliness, but I had tried to speak, and he found new ways to deprive me and so I withered again, and I couldn't tell them I withered again, I couldn't tell them about The Voices that told me of how I had betrayed the beautiful ones who had read my words and turned their faces to the Son, the ones that told me this fumble would snap their stems and scatter their petals, the ones that told me to start the fire, the ones that told me that I deserved to *burn*.

>Back.
>Forth.
>Back.
>Forth.

It was 6am.

The first time I heard The Voices was way before I was unLYSHed. Before my body was first bitten. Even before him. And they didn't start with the thoughts of pursuing Death before Death came for me; they used to subtly whisper that I would always be alone.

It was interesting that they would speak those words and even more so that somewhere in my heart, I believed them. Love had always been around me. It was in the carpets and the pipes of the homes where I grew up, it left its imprint in each step my parents took, it branded me from the hugs my brothers and I would share, it ran through my veins as I was a product of true love, and Love had *bled* for me. I believed in its reality—and in its ability. I wanted it to *fill* me—but the whispers exposed something deep within me that I hid under mounds of insecurity and much later, inside The Only Man I Ever Wanted to Call *"Baby;"* more than I *knew* Love, I trusted *Fear*.

It was 6am.

I looked for answers as I rocked.

How does new wine find itself in old wineskins? What drove a better version of me backward, but that underlying doubt, that intimidating thought that there was no love better for me? Ever present and in power was the Fear of nothing *more*—which meant to avoid being alone, I had to take what I had or what I was closest to and turn it into something… passing. Not something good. So I took him, The Only Man I Ever Wanted to Call "*Baby,*" who should have been the one, because he was good enough, and I had said so, and he was there, and I had chosen him, and I gave him everything without asking him to prove anything, like I used to do when I was a little girl, when I would be in one uncle's arms and the other would reach for me, one hand open, the other a closed fist, suggesting that I could get what was inside if I came to him, so I dove into his arms, and there would be nothing in the fist, but I didn't care really, because I loved my uncles, and I wanted them to chuckle like they did when one of them won me from the other, and I wanted us to do it again, so I could make the other uncle just as happy, because my uncles loved me, and it was safe to go to them when they reached for me even if nothing was in their fists, because they would never hurt me or leave me, and I thought that because he, The Only Man I Ever Wanted to Call "*Baby,*" used to see no one in the room but me before he resented everything about me, was born of good people, and had been taught Who God was, and used to look like my equal, and said that we needed our chance, and that he would always love me, and that I could trust him, and that he wasn't coming with nobody else, and that it would be just him, I could dive into his arms without checking to see what was in his fist, like I used to do with my uncles, so I thrust all I was and all I had become into him, The Only Man I Ever Wanted to Call "*Baby,*" and he ripped himself apart, like old wineskin, and showed me what was underneath his polished pretense, and everything there despised me, and I felt it, and I should have checked to see if he meant what he said, or if something was in his fist or maybe I should have realized that he was not a man that loved me, and not listened to him at all, but The Only Man I Ever Wanted to Call "*Baby*" did what my uncles would never, he cast me from his arms and tried to stuff me back into my cage, and it took Dangerous Prayers to gel together my revelation with understanding. Where there is Fear, there is no trust, and not in myself; not in The Only Man I Ever Wanted to Call "*Baby,*" but in the One Who Had Made Me New.

unLYSHed

                                    Back.
    I had been a pathetic believer.
                                    Forth.
    And I should burn for that, too.
    It was 6am.
    At 6am, the sun was just peeling back the covers of night, opening his eyes slowly, but my wrath had already been hard at work.
    At 6am, I had made it from the bed where I lay at night wishing for sleep, but instead only filled my sheets with my sweat and my loathing.
    At 6am, I found my seat in my rocking chair by my bedroom window, pulled myself up into its base, and kissed my knees with my mouth.
    At 6am, the rest of my house had begun to stir from their sweet dreams, but I had already been rocking.
                                    Back.
                                    Forth.
    At 6am, I had become accountable to the point of judgment and turned on myself.
    At 6am, I had already died a thousand deaths in my body—my head had already swarmed with a thousand reasons as to why this should be so.
    At 6am, my soul was fully ablaze and moaning loudly in my ears from the fire I had started, though from my mouth, I never made a sound.
    There was only the rocking.
                                    Back.
                                  Forth.
It was 6am.

wrath

my daddy says
*"you cannot play russian roulette
with an automatic weapon."*
i tell him
*tell that to the voices hissing
otherwise in my head*

-     *they're back*

unLYSHed

i can birth whole galaxies from my
grief
places where the trees grow from
the sky
where the fruit of the vine is sour
grapes and teardrops
places that smell like soiled diapers
and rotten fruit
places where flowerheads are
human skulls
places where the wind whistles the
sorrows in goodbye
cities are ruined as i groan
the grass grows in red
it is
a wonderful wasteland
everything about this place
is wrong

and you let him?
they ask
it is as natural an occurrence as a
woman's monthly flow
it is as effortless a task as falling in
love
it is as expected a thing as to find
dishes in the cabinets
it's been impossible to change the
course
i scold him
i forgive him
i wipe his slate clean
he is convinced he is God's gift
and maybe even God Himself
i'm locked in a time loop
before him
in prayer posture
before he
chops off my head
the cycle starts again
i keep coming back

-     *enabling*

unLYSHed

i am having quality time with my love
my body is bare
my hands are raised toward heaven
he has tied them together with pink satin scarves
he whispers
let's make a masterpiece
long strokes
of memories devouring another woman
deep strokes
of things for which he resents me
because i am not
short strokes
for the time he spent wishing i'd be undone
he finger paints a smile on my face with the blood from my back
his creation
drips down the length of my body
and runs onto the floor
he snaps at me
you're making a mess
i tug at the scarves
the weight of my
battered body
pulls me to the floor
from my knees, i make a bowl with my arms
i stop the blood flow and pull the paint
stolen from inside my body
back towards myself
i turn to face him as a caramel cherry swirl
perfumed with pennies
and reach for his hand
i say,
can you help me to the bath
his face becomes a cinnamon twist
contorted with frowns and disgust
he pats me on the back
one
two
three
he turns to leave
quality time is over

i quickly look for myself in his painting
an outline for the times he begged me to wait
a brush stroke for the times he begged me to return to him
i am nowhere to be found
not honored in his memory
or in his artwork
as he leaves me to clean myself
he turns back and says
for now
this is the only way i can love you
he closes the door
i shave my head

impossible stains:

worth:
The unLYSHed definition of the term was: inherent, immeasurable, irrevocable **value**. But to whatever version of myself I existed as presently, it had disguised itself as incomprehensible. Inaccessible. Even if it was mine, my connection to it was weak, and I shouldn't have been available while dressed in worthlessness. The look only helped me draw a particular bunch of suitors. Like the ones that wore nice suits and looked nice in suits. And who feigned success. And who smiled for cameras but who never smiled at me. And who behind closed doors, told me where my worth went and how it was never coming back. And how badly I needed them to even get close to it. And how having them meant giving to them. How the price was bone and blood and body. And how they didn't have to ask for it. And how they didn't ask for it. How they could just take it. Because that's how love worked. With me doing all the giving and all the losing only to find that bone and blood and body and name and mind and time and all wasn't enough for me to earn their giving. That I had to *earn* their giving. And how I believed them. And how I had to get back what I had lost, and so I became a giver. And how I gave them grace and time and loyalty and silence for them and me to **be**. And how I did my best to be exactly what they wanted. Even though it cost me my fingertips. Even though it cost me my teeth. And how the process of becoming theirs made my need for them grow. And how soon it was bigger than my entire body. How it was bigger than I thought my worth ever was. How I became consumed with being right for *them* so I could get back to my worth. Or just close to it. because I believed them when they said, "*It's gone—***and it's never coming back."**

***

The Only Man I Ever Wanted to Call "*Baby*" had indeed been a consumer of souls.

I was only one woman cramped into his belly—only one of the many who had lost gaps of life and gaps of self in his badland of body, both in bondage and in love with *him*.

Once we were inside his voids, we had lessons.

One: Take off your shoes before you step onto the carpet.

Two: Keep your belongings arranged neatly in the second room.

Three: Ask him nothing.

Four: Give to him without question.

Four: But don't be too eager.

Four: That's what makes him stay.

Four: That's what makes him want you more.

Four: Until he changes the rules.

Five: Your fight is with each other.

Five: Not because he says so, but because

Five: When he's with you, he compares you to her.

Five: He tells you *how* to be you.

Five: How to be the you that *he* likes.

Six: Learn to share your space.

Six: Learn to share your piece of him.

Six: Accept when he must be with one longer than he can be with the other.

Six: Deal with your own betrayal on your own time when he leaves one bed for another.

Six: He will leave one bed for another.

Six: But you had better not.

Seven: Have your face fixed when he returns.

Eight: Lest he leave again.

Eight: Lest he give another your portion of his time.

Nine: Keep home ready for him.

Ten: Be waiting with all forgiven for when he decides to return.

Ten: When *he* decides to return.

Ten: *If* he decides to return.

It was true that for me, he had always *"returned."* A fact in which I held no honor because it meant that he had *always* either hidden me away or let me leave, and I used to think I was being a big woman, giving him ultimatums, turning my back on him when he let me down, not realizing I was only giving up my then time to step back into my cage, in waiting for the next moment where he would call to me. Want me. But this time, I gave the exiting power to *him*. I was experiencing *his* departure, and I felt as though I had been plucked out of his body and spat from his mouth, with him abhorred by the taste of me. Cast out, covered in saliva, haunted by empty questions and dial tones and insults of exes that ain't my exes, I felt my own repugnance stirring. Some for my actions and for myself—but an abundance for him and the kind of goodbyes he gave. The ones that never actually said "goodbye" but rather scuttled around the term like cockroaches that run from light. Nonetheless, he had gone.

And I was done.

It was *strange*—to look at him with more rage than longing. More grief than acceptance. To find that my body was resisting the cycle—that the thoughts in my head were telling me to defy his rules and…to start another fire. One for his body, much like the one consuming mine.

The absence of that familiar desire for him created a newness in me. Our endings used to turn me to tears; his discard and disappearing act turned me to *darkness*. My subconscious reminded me constantly that the blame for my present was on me—the dream was always the same.

Me, lying alone in the middle of his bedroom floor, trying to come to my feet. My eyes set on his bedroom door, which he had left ajar. His footprints that led up the hallway lined in deep red. The crimson pattern that embellished the ivory fabric of his apartment floor. The putrid, unforgettable scent of sweat and salt and rusted metal. Then there was the shock. The increase in my heart rate as I realized how much blood I had lost. Me realizing… I had no idea how much blood I had lost. The sight of my back. The no longer unblemished flesh, now shredded, sliced, and burning with pain. The need to breathe and not vomit. The need to vomit. Again and again. The lack of ability in my legs. The impossibility of standing or sitting up. The relentless taunting of my thoughts as I accepted he had left me there all night to sleep in my blood because I hadn't learned the rules. That if he said it didn't happen, then I didn't get to stand my ground. If he said I made it up, that meant I must have remembered incorrectly. Even if I still had the scars. Even if I wrote it all down. Even if he had copies and time-stamped receipts. That I shouldn't have argued. That I shouldn't have made my point. That I shouldn't have been where he had asked me to be because I should have known that what he said wasn't what he meant yet. And that he wasn't ready still. And what I had just gotten—all the reasons he couldn't love me *today* beaten into my flesh—was *my* fault. That I needed to fix it. That I needed to move. That I needed to thank him for the pink scarves he used to bind my wrists because he thoughtfully remembered my favorite color. That I needed to thank him for the quality time because he didn't have to give me anything at all. That I needed to show him I was grateful, and that I would fight for him and that I would wait for him. I needed to get up off my belly. I needed to get his floor cleaned…

***

Clean Up Day was a ceremonious event growing up. Gospel music filled the house. Mama's feet would cross the kitchen floor and simultaneously serve as our alarm clocks. Me and the boys would come running. We would play in the Woolite because we liked how it foamed up like shaving cream. We sprayed way too much Pledge on the coffee tables and belly-flopped from the stairs right onto all the pillows that were supposed to be nestled into the sofa. Then, Mama would get on to us, but it would be through a smile because she loved to see her kids be kids. Loved to see that nothing stole away our innocence while we slept. Loved how my brothers and I made our own worlds of play in everything around us. Then we would sing along with the music and put the living room back in order. Then we would finish the kitchen. Mama washed the dishes and I rinsed. My lil' brother dried and put the dishes away. My big brother wiped off the table, and the baby would go for the broom that was bigger than him. He would think he was helping, and we'd tell him, "Good job, Baby." He would put the broom down so I could get it. Then I would sweep. Then Mama mopped. We would wipe and wash and spray and burn a candle when it was all done. Then the house would glisten. And Daddy would come home from work and say, "Look at all the work y'all did. The house looks good, Bae. Y'all did a great job," and me and the boys would sit at Daddy's feet and look at our hard work. At how nothing was out of place—how everything was in order. How it was like a mess had never happened. How that meant we had done *good*.

The Only Man I Ever Wanted to Call "*Baby*" wanted me to be as soulless as the tile on our kitchen floor. The pans that slept under the stove. The pillows on the backs of our sofas. He wanted to keep leaving me in a mess and come home one day and find everything in order; find me *glistening*. Like he and I had never torn the wallpaper, broke the glass, or cracked the windows. Like the threads of the carpet didn't hold my pleading. Like my back wasn't bloodied. Like my heart hadn't rolled under the bed. Like my mind wasn't lost. Like my LYSH wasn't lost. All he wanted for me to do was *glisten*. All he wanted for me to be was *good*.

For a long time, I tried to be what he wanted.

I tried to be cleaned up each time he came back for me.

But I couldn't be soulless.
Couldn't keep hiding the messes.
Couldn't *clean* the wrath.
Couldn't silence the moans.
Couldn't find forgiveness.
For him or for me.
The stains were impossible.
I couldn't get them out.
I couldn't get them out.

unLYSHed

"on your knees"
you say
'open your mouth'
you demand
i should have crowed of my disdain
for your allergen to authenticity
instead, i create the scary sight
of a brainless, thoughtless slave
i kneel before you in obedience
jaw dropped
waiting
for you to fill my throat with
retribution for daring to speak out
the petals were sauteed with honey
the stems
seasoned with lemon and herb
the same gift i so carefully prepared
before declaring
"it's ready,"
is the gift you are forcing me to
swallow
this course of savory actuality
doubled as our last supper —
the only meal that could possibly
bring us back to one another for
better
after we had created
worse
instead of letting the flavors take
you on a necessary ride
instead of even showing me to the
door
you stand over me
dish in hand
and fork your servings back into my
mouth
with no time to catch my breath
to control the gagging
or to wipe my tears
you show me without speaking
your love for me is as i wrote it
you create your own way
to make me eat my words

-         *the sunflower project*

she is a picture of lost life
a polaroid of broken vows
a still shot of the bait that had her hooked
the things he claims to have never said
the things he declares he never meant
he didn't know
gaslighting can wake the dead
be a gentleman
welcome your guest
'the woman from beyond the grave'
don't you remember
you left a decade inside her belly
she carried every year to term
but none made it to life
you, love
bombed her womb
your seeds are strangled by her umbilical cord
they drag the ground behind her
and hang like knots in ribbon from between her thighs
they look just like their father
they want to see you, too
rose thorns pin her veil in place
grass stains
embellish her tattered gown
her arms are full with memorabilia
the gifts you gave
the letters you wrote
the things that rested with her in the earth
your teeth marks tattoo her breasts
your skin and sweat
are under her fingernails
there are planks in the sockets for her eyes
one of love
one of worship

she smiles as she speaks your name
she leans in as she approaches
it's been so long
she smells like you
your mama's house and laundry detergent mixed with her own decay
won't you kiss her now ?

unLYSHed

with fire
and knife
i am freeing my heart's chambers
of your fingerprints

there you are
the real you
a man turned into a mouse
a mouse pretending to be a man
you show your true self when you
are cornered
your disrespect was still hanging in
the air
it was a heavy musk
with notes of malice and narcissus
for two days, i would inhale
and puke
my weak stomach and my hysteria
must have been unattractive
another fault of mine that is no fault
of yours
*the more you want me, the less i
want you* you said
and i thought you were to die for
that night i let my unanswered
questions off the leash
i mutated
to you, i must have appeared to be
too
awake
how dare i ask a master manipulator
for truth
you transfigured before my eyes
and scurried behind my bed
i tried to catch you
i called to you
i beat the floorboards with my hands
i realized you weren't coming back
i pressed my face into my vomit
i boiled the water for my bath
i started the fire for my feet
i sharpened the razors for my thighs
tonight, i would be punished for
trusting you again
and then
i would catch a mouse

i busied myself with my "knew
better" ritual
and was startled by the removal of
my front door
did you tell her where i lived
did you let her
read our love letters
how can she know to talk to me like
you do
you are cowering again
crawling up her leg and
hiding in her breast pocket
it turns out she likes mice
she smiles as she takes in the smell
of my burning soles
she looks at me and asks
did he hurt you again?

unLYSHed

there is a madman raging through
my bloodstream
he sheds his skins of venom
they nest in my veins
they change my heart
i become a cottage
small
secluded
a home for one
vengeance takes up much space
jars of preserves fill my cupboards
they are
labeled: *compassion*
labeled: *empathy*
labeled: *forgiveness*
i do not have a taste for them
maybe i'll nibble on them later
dinner is ready
i'm having a delicacy
slow-cooked jerk tongue and hip
bones
can i offer you a bite?
have a seat
look around
do you like what i've done with the
place?
the wallpaper is custom-made
it is studded with teeth
the dining table's centerpiece made
with real lung
i did it all myself
i am consumed with their jeering
they laugh at my sorrow
i am tortured by their togetherness
they blind me with their closeness
i decided to make better use of their
smiles
this way, we can all continue to be
soul-tied
and now
i can be the homemaker he wanted

guilty:

I was hoping to enter heaven without blood on my hands.
That hope and my forearms down to my fingertips were now all stained red, and guilt lured over me like the blade of the guillotine, ready to satisfy my longing to see blood spill.

To see heads roll.

I'd probably have to lose my hand to get my lick back, but I considered it from the chopping block; whether it'd be worth it to shed blood to cause a bleed.

I loved this new me.

I despised this new me.

Loved because instead of crying, instead of masking, and instead of turning cheeks, she wanted to do something to those who had done something to *me*.

Despised because instead of trusting, instead of forgiving, and instead of turning cheeks, she wanted to do something to those who had done something to *me*.

Decisions, decisions.

Mama had raised me and my brothers by the mantra she had learned from her father. The mantra he had learned from his mother. She told us to love God. To love people. To be *sweet*. The LYSH I wanted to be had the heart to do it. To love God. To love people. To be sweet. Like Mama said. Like Granda wished. In a way that would make Great-grandma Ella smile. In some ways, in some seasons, with some souls, I had done it. I had seen straight through people to their bubblegum center—where they were the sweetest. The softest. I held people long enough to feel their heartbeats settle—long enough to let them know they were safe for as long as a hug in my arms could last. I made time to listen. I dealt with people with respect to the fact that they weren't big. Weren't small. Just God's. And living. My LYSH smiled. My LYSH *loved*. The hardest. The deepest. In a way that was sweet. In a way that always endured.

That LYSH pleased me—I believed that that LYSH pleased God.
But I was convinced early in my life that that LYSH didn't make me *enough*.
She didn't make my friends want to continue to be my friends.
She didn't make The Only Man I Ever Wanted to Call "*Baby*" love me better, love me, alone, or love me lastingly.

I loved that LYSH, but the ones whose love I wanted, didn't.
That LYSH was no good at "outgrowing" or "goodbye."
So instead of cutting ties, I cut myself—down.
Back.
Off.
Away.

I don't think I ever decided consciously that I would choose acceptance over identity—but I do remember the season when I decided I wanted to be *liked*. I couldn't have been older than 8. Didn't realize that in the same moment, I became guilty of a crucifixion. Or that I waged a war of Me vs. Me that I would fight for 20 years. I had no idea—but before I knew anything about what it meant to be LYSH, I had folded up a great deal of my body, my opinions, my permission, and my essence and hid them in the back of my closet. Underneath the faces I needed to wear to be wanted. To be liked. To be *loved*.

And yet, here I was alone.
Wearing 40 times 4 heartbreaks' worth of other people's skin.
Still without other people's love.
It was why I wanted to see blood spill.
Why I wanted to see heads roll.

Vengeance wasn't another mask I was merely fitting to my face—he had a soul. And his own skin. *And he had snuck into my blood.*

I hadn't known Vengeance, but maybe I should have housed him sooner; back when my 5th grade crush pushed me into our class set of ELA desks or when my 6th-grade-bully started a riot meant to burn me alive, rallied behind her the black kids in our class because, in her words "everybody thinks she's perfect, but she's not perfect," or the first time The Only Man I Ever Wanted to Call "*Baby*" was caught with another woman in his hands and on his leash. Maybe instead of absorbing the maltreatment, lacing my lips with apology for a wrong that wasn't identified, sacrificing my respect, or thinking the problem was *me*, I should have met every threat and every foe with a balled fist.

A switchblade.
A match.

It seemed that after years of fumbled opportunities to self-protect or self-defend, I had found myself at self-destruct—the prerequisite for revenge—and it was all I could think of when her words slit my throat.

16

A girl I did not know but who spoke like she and my shame went way back.

A girl whose entrance I had barred but whom The Only Man I Ever Wanted to Call "*Baby*" brought into me through my windows and his judgements.

A girl whom I had seen inside of him. A girl I had shared scraps with from my cage.

A girl I thought I understood—whom I hadn't judged but had pitied.

A girl who had used her next opportunity to be his to stomp around on my heart shards while holding his hand.

A girl who caught me by surprise because I thought the girl had the same scars as me.

A girl who didn't realize she had the *same scars as me.*

I hadn't had enough time to settle down after his last words and the disconnected phone line. To breathe until I had made his actions okay. To come up with some way to excuse his disrespect before I was face to face with an intruder who stayed long enough to mock me.

When it happened, I think I malfunctioned. All the bodies and all the masks went wild. In one moment, there was the twisted glory of yielding to rage and the spine-crushing disappointment of breaking God's heart. And Grandma Ella's. Maybe it was self-defense—maybe I merely attacked for all the times I never had—but a vengeful LYSH saw her time to destroy and took it. She wanted to see blood spill.

She wanted to see heads roll.

I knew exactly how I got here and had no idea how I had gotten here—in the pit of pure mania. Between what was sweet and what was sinful. Where it wasn't clear what LYSH would do because LYSH had been dunked in acid. Because LYSH had been lost to rejection. Abuse. *Wrath.*
"*Here*" was where wrath caused the skin to rip off of my composure. Where I wanted an eye for my eye. A soul for my soul. And yet, I wanted to be sweet. But I resented being sweet. And I wanted someone to defend me. To choose me. To protect me. And it seemed I had no one to protect me. Where so much of me was hurting. Where all of me was hurting. *Where I desperately didn't want to be the only one hurting.* Where I wished I *could* cause blood to spill. Where I wished I *could* cause heads to roll. But I wasn't good at intentionally hurting another soul. Where I knew I would not unleash my rage, nor could it be silenced or tamed. Where that left my rage

inside of me to rip my gut out of my body and into four sets of four. Where I knew my pain was no one's fault. Especially not a girl I never met. Nor the Only Man I Ever Wanted to Call "*Baby.*" Nor a crush, or a bully, or any other lost soul that needed some grace? Where I couldn't convince myself that *I was a soul that needed some grace*, but it was easy for me to believe that God had left me to suffer. Where the masks tried to consume me. For leaving LYSH unnurtured and unprotected. Where wrath set someone loose inside of me who was feral and dangerous. And not to the ones I'd been hurt by—*only to myself.*

I wanted recompense for my suffering, but the only culprit I could see was me.

The blood on my hands was mine.

For never having said, "This isn't good for *me*," or "*I* deserve much better," or "I'd rather be alone and myself than whatever they want to turn me into."

For being a poor steward of my body and my soul.

For wanting to hurt people that were already hurting and didn't know that they were hurting.

For staying too long in places that rejected me and seeing the worst of those to whom I should have already said goodbye.

For not acknowledging I was worthy long before I met The Only Man I Ever Wanted to Call "*Baby*" or the other women surviving him.

For never allowing myself to be myself without tying myself to shame.

For not starting with God and staying with God.

For not believing that I could be loved without becoming someone tiny.

For folding up my LYSH and hiding her away.

For taking so long to want to be more than "*anyone's.*"

Wrath lowered guilt closer and closer to my neck, with the aim to threaten me.

To end me.
To cause blood to spill.
To cause heads to roll.

they are feasting on my dignity
and You don't even care

- *dear God*

unLYSHed

i use my lipstick to color my face
swirls and loops and swirls and loops
til every feature is covered
i pull my lips from my mouth like velcro
i toss them to the sea
i'd rather be hidden
i'd rather be silent
since i've become an imposter
i say that i am fine
i say that i forgive you
but today i ripped out 4 patches of my hair
i closed a heat press on my head
i want to speak myself into peace
but find my body is armed with my teeth
my fists
loaded with bane
i want to fire them right at you
i shouldn't say that
i'll fix it
i'll feed my fingers to the garbage disposal
i feel the need to rush into "okay"
but my feet have rooted me to the front lawn
how do i move on
the discord between my character
and the beast of wrath itself
is driving me insane
if i cannot hurt you
if i will not hurt you
i should rather
hurt myself

CONSUMED: THE SURVIVOR'S STORY

my doctor is a white man
my visit is routine
i lay on my back
i hike up my dress
he opens her mouth
and swabs behind her lips
he presses down on my stomach
he notices as i squirm
he asks me
does it hurt
i nod my head
yes
he finds it at 7 centimeters
he thrusts his seer into my body to put
eyes on the intruder in my womb
where my children had not yet been was
a growth that stretched the width of
cities
although my body carried it as if it was a
baby
monthly
i would tremble with earthquakes of
cramps and contractions
i would mother the red sea
i would lie
ailing
pinned to the floor, begging God to
allow the pain to pass
to find that after labor
my belly was still full
the doctor swears to me
"it's not alarming."
"if it gets any bigger, we'll see about its removal."

my doctor is a white man
2 years later i visit him again
this visit is routine
i lay on my back
i hike up my dress
he opens her mouth
and tries to swab behind her lips
he pauses
he says,

"i'm struggling to see your cervix
because your fibroid is so big."
he presses down on my stomach
he asks if it hurts
i answer with a moan and a roll of my
head
when he spoke again
it was not before he tapped fear on its
shoulder
and welcomed it
to wrap me with its tongue
lift me from the ground
and pull me into its throat belly first
he said *there will be surgery*
he said *there will be lots of blood*
he said *he was afraid* so he would send
me to someone else
i walked out of the doctor's office
pamphlet clenched in hand
i practiced my new word
"myomectomy"
in shock and in tears
months later
i learned that when he found it at 7cm
i was already showing to be 13 weeks
pregnant with terror
my womb and my body were stretching
themselves thin
trying
to give it more room
he found it at 7cm
it would be extracted at 10
along with the two hiding behind the
first
he found it at 7 cm
but he didn't get it out
can someone tell me
why didn't he get it out

21

unLYSHed

it's like finding a possum under your bed
or termites in your grits
what are you doing here
you frighten me
you disgust me
who let you in
this parasite
that sucks ability from the walls of the womb
that eats at the functionality of the lady place
it is the black woman's plague
and it has made me
sick
no antibiotic will heal me
there is no over-the-counter cure
their best medicine is to make a jack o lantern of my abdomen
into my belly
they want to carve a smile
they say, "this is the only way you may be able to be a mother."
she says, "this is the way that kept me from being a mother."
they corner me with ultimatums
neither looks like freedom
or diapers
or onesies
or mini me's
i close my eyes
i breathe deeply
and become the specimen for their tables
they take my blood
they pump me with iron
i prepare to let them cut away

last night
i dreamed of giving birth to my children
they came out feet first
and had pumpkins for heads

i awakened the house with my screams

my heart had been mangled
i was pregnant with boulders and bricks
and it was not safe for me
to hug my grandmother

-        breaking point

natural birth:

He had given me the news from my least favorite position.
On my back.
My legs raised above my hips.
A stranger between my thighs.
Before, I never screamed.
Before, I never fought.
Instead, while another lost himself within my body, I exited it to hide myself within my mind.
Like how I did with good music.
When I applied what my daddy had taught me.
When we found a new love song, or just a new song with love in it or pain in it or happy in it, and he would ask me, "Have you heard…?"
And I'd say, "No sir."
And we'd find it somewhere.
And we'd listen to it together.
And we'd play it enough to learn it.
And we'd learn it well enough to sing it.
And we'd sing it, with our eyes closed and our heads thrown back, and a snap between our fingers, and a slight dip in our brows, and a bob on our heads, and we'd be lost for the minutes it took the song to play, hidden in our own stories and in our own minds, as we listened to the sounds with a soul, and made sounds with a soul.
My escape had been in my head.
In my music.
To my daddy.
But when I found myself in my least favorite position—
On my back.
My legs raised above my hips.
A stranger between my thighs.
I was alone.
Convinced I couldn't run to my Daddy.
So, I ran inside myself.
To the place where I made music.
And I would sing.
And I would *lie*.

I would fantasize my next moments as the lyrics of my favorite love songs, like "See You in the Morning" for when he finished, and "When Can I See You Again" before he left, and "Play Another Slow Jam," when he finally learned my name, and "Thank You in Advance" for when he discovered that I was loveable, I thought of any song that would tell me this wasn't what it was, any song that bleeped out coercion, and date rape, and assault, something that would keep me out of the mood of beating them out of my blood, or that could teach me not to blame myself for not screaming, not fighting, because maybe two months from now, I could bury this moment where I didn't say "yes," under heaps of intimacy and commitment and I would never think of it again because I
could... "make him love me."
And love would help me forget.
And love would later give me babies.
And I would stay until I made it so.

I was never able to make it so.

That was why I was afraid, and Fear had driven me to misuse love songs.
To be desperate for love because love could stop the strangers.
To sit in the confusion alone to avoid the judgment.
To the lie that no one could help me.
To the lie that God would be ashamed.

I had come to learn quite a bit about God for myself, but I had also heard many people speak as though they knew Him, too. Their talks about the marital act started with "wait til marriage" and ended with "the consequence of sexual sin," and they may have known God, but a lot of 'em didn't know *me*. How I absorbed wrongdoings. How I accepted maltreatment as something I brought upon myself. How when I sat up in my bed alone after a night of hiding and singing, my first thoughts were never on the nurturing my body needed. I didn't give my soul hugs. I thought about the church folk, who, if they knew, would ask me, "How many have you been with?" as if there's always a clear decision to "be with" somebody. I thought about the shaking fingers in front of the "had you not slept with him," as if it's always your decision to lay next to somebody, and how that insinuation was leading to how if I had been a better mystery maybe a man would want me more—treat me better. As if I had to be something that motivated him to be the man his mama raised. Then there were the assumptions—the "that would never be you, you know better than to be here or going there or doing this and saying that," like I wasn't a girl like every other girl, like I wasn't supposed to be able to go anywhere at whatever time and have the right to be left alone, or like my tongue would always work right or that it would never be removed from my mouth, or like I had enough power or enough strength in my mind or my fists to beat a grown man back into his place, a place that was far away from my legs, or like I had been exposed to every kind of manipulation in the world, and that I was meant to know how to be quicker than that before I turned 16. Or 19. Or 25.

All of their reflections made what had happened in the night my fault, and that made what happened in the night my responsibility to fix. My fixing made things worse, and I thought now, as the doctor I thought I knew let stress cast a shadow over his face, busy at work between my thighs, that maybe I had put my body in harm's way. Maybe the stale seed that didn't turn into babies hardened itself inside of me and expanded. Maybe I had been carrying my guilt and bad teaching in more than just my eyes. Maybe it was in my womb too. And as the doctor struggled to find his words, I realized that "it" was in the way of my future. My family. My *babies*.

It seemed as though my desire for motherhood was cultivated with my consciousness. I never knew a time in my heart or in my head since I knew of my heart and of my head that I didn't long to fill both my heart and my head with my love for my children. I had seen them clear as *day* in my dreams, their features alike my own, except for their noses and complexion. They were quite apparently *mine*—bone of my bone. Flesh of my flesh. Always on my mind but never in my arms. Close to me in my subconscious but unfathomable in my reality.

Although love was missing from my love life, there had been no lack of ignorance or carelessness, and still—there were no babies. I wasn't necessarily *looking* for them before I met the man who would be My Safe Place to Land, but their absence led me to wonder about my *body*. What she was good for—who's side she was on. If everything about her was okay. If she had been traumatized by the strangers. If I had broken her and received the consequence of sexual sin like the church folk had said or if... I was merely experiencing mercy. How without love, I would never really know.

unLYSHed

But I had believed that God could see the shades of gray in the nights something happened in the night. And it was God that had stopped the strangers. I had hoped my body would listen to reason. I had hoped she would learn to forgive me. I had hoped she would unfold herself to me and my dream could become *our* dream again. I had hoped that at my annual check-up, she might have left a message for me—that all was well. That all was healed. That all was forgiven.

But when the stranger between my thighs pulled his utensils out of my lady place, he dragged a name from his lips across his brow, drenched in a fear of his own.

The name was not victory.

The name was not good news.

He ended our relationship that day with the "it's not you, it's your fibroid," and made plans to pass me along to another. Someone who could treat me better, who could meet my needs, who could—
Give me what I deserved.

As he exited the examination room, I didn't scream.

I didn't fight.

I dressed and came to my feet.

I stumbled out of his office and fell into song.

A *boom* from the impact of my knees in the concrete.

A *shhh*—from my fingernails scraping against the gravel.

Mmmm for the bass as I lay in the lot defeated.

Clashing notes in the treble from the gasps and grunts I released when I was finally ready to lift my body from the ground.

I took my place in the driver's seat and kept the beat with long breaths and head taps against the steering wheel.

I birthed a troubled composition.

It told the tale of a LYSH—

With no faith.

With no love.

With no babies.

But with bodies.

And still with bondage.

And pasts that couldn't be escaped.

Who heard voices that wouldn't be silenced.

Who carried threats that tormented her womb.

Threats that terrorized her *dream*.

The dream had been to be hand in hand with My Safe Place to Land—contracting and pushing and waiting and listening *for the purest sound with soul.*

The first song sang by the little bodies that were to come from *my* body. Like I had seen in my dreams. The ones who were

> bone
> of my bone.
> flesh
> *of my flesh.*

unLYSHed

the world has turned upon itself
the sun and stars declare war
the earth and the sky
eat each other alive
the wind is infectious
to touch is to sin
and my state of mind
has forgotten its boundary lines
it has stepped into the territory of insanity
it has spilled over onto hopelessness
it has stretched into anxiousness and revolutionized
to change its name to pain
i have many questions
i wonder where my Daddy is
i wonder why He left us here
i wonder
who will pay for this

-        *when they said 'pandemic'*

behind my bedroom door
i scale my walls
i crawl above my window
i hang from my ceiling upside down with my face turned toward the day's light
my forehead is burned by my carpet as i swing
and i hum
here is where i watch the virus turn backyards into gravesites
my blood rushes to my head
i imagine what it would be like
to be a sparrow
to be clueless to the madness invading the earth
i wonder if i would like the taste of worms and insects
yesterday, i tried to write
and my left hand strangled me
yesterday, i tried to smile
my daddy tested positive
yesterday, i tried to forget
last night, i attended their wedding in my nightmares
so today
i will hang here
til the blood rushes to my head
i will swing
til i remove all of the skin on my face
i will watch as the world is turned into God's acre
i will pray that it does not welcome my daddy for 8 o'clock service
for dinner
i'll try birdseed
deep fried

unLYSHed

my pillow is the catching mitt for all of my screams

i try to sing myself lullabies
but my tunes are better suited for horror films
i didn't know i could make such sounds
that i could be
the villain and the victim
i say to myself
but i love you
my reflection spits in my face
some part of me hates to be told lies
that's my heartbeat you hear
when i'm asked a question, i panic —
it's because i don't know the answer you wish for me to give
i think i left my fortitude in my mother's womb
i need a new one
i'm not hiding
i'm trying to find a way to stop hurting myself
my body has become a vortex that sucks in the unkind
my mind has wandered away again
will i die this way
with everything in me broken

unLYSHed

as long as wrath wins
    i don't.

woe

if you keep burying what needs to be healed
it will grow arms and break through the earth
it will steal you from your bed
it will rip you apart
it will
eat you alive

dear diary,

woe abducts me from wrath and holds me hostage in its mouth. i sit just between its teeth and its tongue, waiting.
trembling.
trying to steady my breath.
there are bones here. they are all that is left of my desires. woe snacks on them at night. the fight i had in wrath is packed in its jaws. the back of its throat is painted with my face.
i have been quiet.
i haven't moved for days.
i try not to make a sound, but woe knows i am here.
woe knows where it keeps me.
the walls finally begin to break down. woe salivates. its belly grumbles. it readies itself for its dinner. **it prepares to consume me**.

unLYSHed

it would be a baritone note
shimmying in minor feel
powerful enough to make this earth rattle
but my pain is not a sound
there would be smoke
thick like sheep's wool
if my mind were to become burning curtains
in a crumbling house
the people living within
would shriek in high frequencies
and transform the contents in my head into confetti
pop
what's going on with you
they ask
i could tell them
pick a door
any door
behind door number one
is ammo for tsunami waves
last night my eyes poured another gallon into the supply
door number two
my closet
i stitched a wardrobe out of my prayer pages
my soul is a watermelon slice
to the devil trapped behind my skin
behind door number three
he feeds
what's going on with you
they ask
i could tell them
pick a door
instead, i remain silent
i refuse to let them see
what is happening to me

-       *consumed*

the marching feet of a thousand men is my new haunting
the enemy's camp smells like the dead
he's made me their trophy
captured
stripped
and strung up by my toes
raised above all of his subjects
my skin
he stole
to make their flags
with strands of my hair, he sewed their emblem
i've dangled here for days
where is my Protector
i do not feel worthy
with my sins under microscope
my fragility displayed for all to see
his followers mock me
they lick my bleeding wounds
they spit upon my flayed body
their laughter is laced with hate
i want my rescue
i want God to unhinge my body from this post
to hide my nakedness with His wings
to fly me home
and to burn this place to the ground
i give my supplications to the wind
i entwine them with the desperation of the woman with the issue of blood
pump them with the wailings of Job
and seal them with the prayer of the Savior
why have you forsaken me

unLYSHed

they rush in with wash bins teeming with steamy water for my feet
they rush in with terry cloth to place against my head
they do what they know for the sick and shut-in
they wonder why i do not approach "better"
oh, you sweet, bustling souls
fussing over my bed
don't you know
my imagination is fevered and delirious
my memory is wheezing and chilled
your remedies for my body
do nothing for my mind
this sickness
cannot be seen as sweat beads and runny noses
it cannot be treated with herbs and steam from brewing tea
my head is ill with the infection that poisons my good sense
perception
and reason
there is no cure for this in grandma's purse

-    *mental health awareness*

they tire of watching me grieve
what's the big deal? they ask
is she not over it yet? they gossip
i know i live amongst those who will never know me again
they do not understand
i bear the love i cannot give
the identity i cannot actualize
the life i thought i could create
like a cross on my back
i am one with the splinters in my spine
they are the ones who have never been broken like this

unLYSHed

some days i do try.
i take my cross and drag my fingernails against the wood.
i attempt to carve out a new load.
something less heavy.
something that suits me.
i give it all i have — i work, and i shape and i ask til my nailbeds
are bloodied and rugged.
rejection has been my return.
it comes in silence.
it comes in avoidance.
my portion looks back at me, unchanged, and i'm right where i had
hoped i never would be.
face to face with my last professed fear.
stuck.
still.
where no one sees me.
no one hears me.
no one wants me.
and i can do **nothing** *to save myself.*

each time he said
"i love you"
he dangled it over my head as the last scrap of meat before a famine
maybe he would drop it
if i could earn it
it trembled and ended in question and still
i needed it more than i needed to feel my own heartbeat
if he would let go
i would devour it like the ration he made it to be
it's been months now
my ribcages are showing
my traitorous skin
pants for him
my pores
are open-mouthed and dribbling
if i clog them with shea butter and ink pens
will that stop the longing
if i cut them out completely
will i desire him no more

unLYSHed

the bones in my wrists have been ground to white powder
my forearms are the candlesticks in the chandelier
the pathways in my palms cannot find you
since i cannot hold you, i can hold nothing
where should my love for you go
should it hide itself in the bottom rim of my eye
should it dive into our last polaroid print
should it disappear in the threads of your tshirt resting in my top drawer
this grief
sinks its teeth into my neck
it pumps its poison down to my toenails
if i am not yours
i am lost
if there is no us
who do i become
no part of me knows how to forget you
and yet, with you gone
my affections are
homeless
and too great to be left alone with me

if i were to touch you

you'd become a porcupine
a shark's tooth
a snake's bite
and acid rain

the things that would harm me

if i were to need you

you'd turn into silence
an empty bed
and home
and hospital room

the ways and places you left me

if i were to want you

you'd turn into sewage pipes
rat droppings
a bowl of maggots

the things that disgust me

if i were to love you

you'd turn into wind chills
four knuckles
a broken skull
a perverted heart

incapable of giving love back to me

unLYSHed

it's like a hiccup on pause
the breath is frozen
roadblocked
it is denied access both to fill me and to exit me
so, it balls itself into a fist of wind gusts
and violates my sternum
i stab me from the inside
shanked by my own bone
my heart loses its blood
my body loses its nerve
feeling hitchhikes away from my toes
my skin goes gray
veins bulge from my eyes
the duffels beneath them carry the color of midnight ocean blue
my lips
peel like onion skin
the fist grows larger
hits harder
determined to fulfill its duty
demanding
that breath be allowed to pass
and when i do
breathe
when pause becomes play
and the extended inhale
becomes a cadence of sucks and blows
as oxygen is shoveled back into my body and my blood
my body shudders and sweats
i fall to my knees
ease onto my face
rub it against the hardwood
and remember
though i'm relieved to be breathing
i'm still alone

-       *loneliness*

depression kinda reminds me of what happens when tea bags hit hot water. how their contents stain the liquid. how the bag is a soggier, heavier, weaker version of itself. i feel like the tea bags. like i've been dunked into life, and the connection between my body and its waters motivates life to feed on me. and so, it does. it sucks the moisture out of my skin. it sucks the hope out of my eyes. it draws on the **believe** *in my spirit, and i can feel them all leaving my body. running out of me. it's the same kind of uncomfortable as getting blood drawn, but intensified, as if there was a needle in every vein and they each pull at one time. depression pulls the good but leaves the heavy. all the love i don't know what to do with. the pain from everything being inside out. the hurt from being left to face my fears alone. the shame from failing over and over and over again. and i'm just* **there**. *as something wrong manifests where my mind and soul collide. diluted. wet. with the space around me thick with everything i'm missing. everything that should be in me, that i can't grab or reinsert, and i* **would** *want it back. but i can't* **want**. *even want floats around me. even want has escaped me, too. so, i keep oozing. of everything that makes me powerful. everything that makes me strong. everything that looks like life. i just sit as it leaves me.*

unLYSHed

trauma opens fire
it scatters my identity and composure like refugees in search of safety
calm and courage and normalcy have been damaged
what was can never be the same again
i unbutton my flesh to look at what's suffering
i find i have spirit wounds
a crime has been committed
wrap me in the yellow tape
chalk the space around my stability
apply pressure
stop the bleeding
will i be okay?
will you
capture the culprit
will you stop her from striking again?

there are memories in my bones
and skin
and body
memories that make me forget how to function
but help me remember how it felt to be victim
there are memories in my bones
and skin
and body
memories i want scooped out of me like the heart of a cantaloupe
memories i want peeled off of me like the skin of a grapefruit
memories i want singed away
memories i want burned into non-existence

unLYSHed

it leads me to slow suck fresh lava through a straw
this turns my teeth to mineral water
makes craters of pus and blister the lie bumps on my tongue
my scalded throat is repaved with scab
my lips
molten
and trapped in eternal pucker
my body is transformed
it's made to become
the holding place for liquid wrath
bring your ear to my belly
that pounding is from my soul
she is trapped inside my body
drowning in my distress
we are turning into layers of rock and ruby
we are hardening from the inside out
day by day
it steals
life

-        *woe*

thursdays are different. on thursdays, i wake up in a hype. my heart rate is up. i want to feel something else. anything else. something that's not me bleeding on the inside. something that's not like i been gutted and my body is screaming and i can't hush her because i can't think because the voices are so loud. the voices never stop speaking. they tell me i can't say i feel like i'm bleeding unless i really know how it feels. to be cut and to let the blood flow. they tell me to stand on it. they tell me to see if it helps. and maybe it's God. that i'm too weighed down to move. or that i'm in my mama's house. and that laughter is on the other side of my door. because i think i would've done it. Because the demons still sneak into my room. they press me into my bed. hiss at me in my sleep. claiming to be God. claiming that there is no way out, but that they can help me pause. they can help me numb. but everything wild and active and audacious in me has seeped out already. had it not—maybe i would've listened. i think i may have listened to the voices when they directed me toward a different type of hurt. one that might distract me. one that would quiet them. at least until the next thursday. when they tell me it's time to hurt myself again.

unLYSHed

i can deep dive into the whites of the clock's face
its hands can row me across the blank sea or
form the anchor that holds me in spacelessness
as long as you stain my lips
as long as you drip from my mouth
i am far away from here
oh, the places we have gone
te moana
for silence
reykjavík
for safety
and i never had to leave my bed
the more of you i consume
the deeper i hide inside my head
where the voices in my thoughts cannot reach me
where the skeletons in my chest cannot pursue me
you are my true love
you are the good feeling i know i can make
last

-            *my bottle of merlot*

on the day you were born
clouds swam through the sky to blow rainwater showers at heaven's gates
a flash mob of angels
performed in the square where our ancestors live
to the music
God tapped His foot
thunder erupted across paradise
shrill and harmonious sounds of excitement
filled the space

there was laughter

on the day you died
angels were caught helping the Son
cleaning a mansion neighboring your great-grandfather's
they carried inside it
riches
they hung a crown above the door
they stood banded across the front yard
arms open
singing
we welcome you home
seconds before you appeared
the angels cried
seconds after you closed your eyes
so did i

unLYSHed

they give me something for the pain
it dissolves behind my lips
relief mixed with the intimidation of the unknown
makes for a strange taste
the worst is over
the best is
unforeseeable
i'm tongue-tied with shouts of
glory
and
woe is me
if i were God
i would whip my hands with 90 lashes
i would make myself kneel in broken glass
i'd harvest my larynx
stick holes in my tongue
i would silence the beggar in me
God gives, and i am unsatisfied
God delivers
and i long for captivity
the israelites must be my forefathers
their fickleness, hereditary
i want to be a mountain of faith
unmoved
and unswerving
instead, i am a grassland
blowing with the wind
strengthless
wavering
it is good that i am not the Merciful
i would show me no mercy
it is good that i am not the Giving
i would close my fist
it is good that i am not God
when my humanity detests me

-          post operation

one night
i positioned my heart for prayer
i closed my eyes tightly
i balled up my body, squeezed my gut
and clenched my fists
a sunflower field bloomed inside of my head
i opened my eyes to find the moon
in the rocking chair by my window
a ribbon was wrapped around it
it was a gift from God
it came with a note
laughter erupted from my throat and frightened me
it had been so long
i smiled
for the first time in months
i grabbed hold of the moon's light
and let myself have a taste
i hadn't had relief
or hope
in quite some time

- *He still loves me*

unLYSHed

i decide to leave my room
i want to see my mama
my family celebrates
they welcome me
mama prepares a feast as i assess the room
i find that my baby brother's body
no longer fits on my back
my big brother's heart has been stolen
right under my nose
my little brother's eyes
still captivate a room, but now
tell tales i have not heard
gray snuck into daddy's beard
mama's face
is sprinkled with fresh freckles
i take my place at the dinner table
a million miles away from those sitting just next to me
those i love the most
i want back in
to be their daughter
their sister
to share in all of the laughs
to know all of the stories
i'm sure they placed me under glass on the mantles of their hearts
still inside of them
but where my love for my hurt could not hurt them so much
i did this to us
and i want it undone
i want life with the living
i want to be here
with them who love me
with them who choose me
not lost to them
consumed
with what was consuming me

shift:

I threw my head back as the water ran over my skin.
Neck.
Chest.
Down to my belly.
I sucked in the steam.
Watched the water droplets consume my new beauty marks.
My battle scars.
The ones left from the procedure that removed the burden from my belly.
The ones that came with stories from my time on the table.
Pinned by the stem.
Like where I was when this all began.
Or rather when it picked up where it left off.
Preparing to undergo God's knife, before I got distracted.
Before I heard someone call my name.
Time had continued to tick while I waited. And suffered. And let Fear have its fill.
Time had been 7 months, and 10 years, and 3 weeks, as I traveled through timelines, to old LYSH's, and roads less traveled, and dead ends, and ends of ropes, and edges of cliffs. The muddy residue from my journey clothed me; I was filthy with impossibility. I was covered in quitting. I had become the most dangerous I had ever been, my toes just over the ledge, when I got distracted. *Someone* called my name.
Louder than The Voices though still still and small.
With more authority than the Only Man I Ever Wanted to Call *"Baby."*
With a strength and a tenderness that blanketed my body in chills.
It was like He was next to me and all over me at the same time, inside of me and leading me all at once. I followed the Sound through corridors and hallways, through wrath and through woe, until I reached the table.
Like where I was when this all began.
Or rather when it picked up where it left off.
Where I was pinned by the stem.
Ready to undergo God's knife.

Before I had gotten distracted.

Before someone who was not This One had called my name.

The goal was to relieve my womb of its heavy load. The process required me to be put under. To visit the place that is so close to death that I would not feel my body being broken into—the entire procedure would begin and end, while I slept.

While I *rested*.

Something I had not done for 7 months. Or 10 years. Or 3 weeks.

Something that had been deprived of me since I got distracted.

Oh, how I had yearned for rest.

It had been nowhere in my travels.

Not in wrath.

Not in woe.

And here it was that through this trauma event on my body, this thing of which I had been terrified, this happening that would plunge me deeper into the unknown—*there was a green pasture.*

A thing my body desperately needed.

That if I wanted to be a mother, I could not avoid.

That to survive mentally and physically, required my faith.

Required my *trust*.

I had to go *through* to get to the green pasture.

I had to go *through* to experience rest.

The operating room should not have been familiar. Nor the tools. Nor the Man. Nor His eyes. Nor His voice. Yet, when He looked at me, I saw my stories on play behind his eyes—my whole life. The 7 months. The 10 years. The 3 weeks. When He spoke to me, He spoke things He should not have known— *"You've been in a great deal of pain."* And when He *touched me*—when He took my hand in His to comfort me before the work began. Or resumed. My hand *fit* into His—stuck to Him magnetically. *Desperately*. Like it knew not to let go. Like it knew it was safe to hold on to Him forever. Like it had known Him before. Like maybe He was rest Himself.

I inhaled deeply as I remembered it all.

As the water ran over my skin.

Neck.

Chest.

Down to my belly.

The first days of recovery had been filled with, "How are you? You feel okay?"

And hugs.

And kisses.

And visits.

And prayers.

But the latter days were almost silent. The perfect environment to listen. To think. To pray. To *remember*.

I had walked around my home like it was both familiar and strange—like I hadn't been there for some time. Like I was coming back slightly changed. But reflecting on what I had shown my walls. What I had given the waters in my bathtub. The secrets I had stuffed into my mattress. The terrors I had hidden under my pillow. In the same space now, were the letters. And the scriptures. And the prayers. And the music. And the sunflowers.

In the valley of the shadow of death there had been wrath.

And woe.

And Fear.

Fear that caused sweats.

Fear that brought The Voices.

And the crossed line denoting insanity.

And fire.

For 7 months. And 10 years. And 3 weeks. And maybe even a lifetime.

And now in the same valley, there were *sunflowers*.

Now, in the same valley I could finally *see* God.

As I threw my head back.

As the water ran over my skin.

Neck.

Chest.

I brought my hands to my belly.

I touched what was healing as my thoughts swarmed. On how strange it was that healing happens after trauma. On how lenses worked. On how when my view is set to wrath, I see fire. And when my view is set to woe, I see ledges. On what might happen if I changed my view to mercy. If I might find that the sunflowers had existed with the flames. If I might find that God had been in the wrath. And in the woe. And in the valley. And that

unLYSHed

He had done that before. Been with me. In the sowing. Been with me. In the withering. And that I had been in the flames, but I had not been consumed. And that I could still feel Sonlight in the shadow of death. And that Fear was not so scary. And if the procedures and the processes were necessary. If more was taken out of me with the invaders of my womb. If there was a gift hidden within the valley. And amidst the flames.

Years ago, I left God's surgical table.

Thinking my life was my own. Thinking that I was going my own way. To find myself right where He wanted me to be.

In the Dwelling Place.

On His table.

Pinned by the stem.

Where He prepared to complete the work He had begun. Where we reconnected. Where we became close. Where He told me He had suffered when I suffered. Where He showed me—*He had scars too.*
He was ready to lead me in how healing was done.

Ready to give me happy.

Ready to make me whole, and it started with me becoming *clean*.

I surrendered as I stood with my head thrown back.
I gave myself to Him and to His process, as the waters ran over my skin.

healing

unLYSHed

>   your surface trauma has a grandmother
>   *go deeper*

this crimson-red loveseat
holds me in its arms
its cushions turn me into
a running faucet of all my secrets
she
sits across from me
she
remains calm
i fill her room with all of my fears
why does that frighten you? she asks
i say
the last man inside me left a seed
my womb choked it out
the last man inside me saw my heart
as his cage
he ripped
and clawed
his way out
the woman inside me is drowning
in almost and maybes
she can't figure out her way out
the God living inside me
is starving
if He were man
even He would want *out*
her glasses float past me as she nods
her understanding
our heads bump the ceiling as the
room reaches its limit
i use my last breath to question her
question
before my secrets suck me under
make it make sense, i implore her
tell me
why hasn't **happy** *already happened
for me*

unLYSHed

my whole head disagrees with itself
my will
like oil
my function
like water
ask me a question, and my insides
will wage war
the dead things still want dominion
they rumble from my belly
but the waters and the vines that live
inside me now
stretch up and through my veins to
nurse me to
ability
they urge me
to command the dead to rest
the riot is beautiful
my glory declares war against my
shame
sunflower skyscrapers crush decay
and rot under their stems
yet
the uprising manifests as confusion
it freezes me in interim pause
i will not know myself
or what i prefer
until the war inside me ends

mind
where are you now
haven't you heard
we're healing
i've packed your bags with scripture
i've left behind your favorite teddy
and tshirt
and lover
i think maybe you've outgrown
them
i think maybe they're too little for
you
i think maybe you don't need the
memories
you know the teddy smells like
smoke
and the tshirt is stained with blood
the love
has evolved
it's lost its potency
it is bland
it is soiled
it is no longer love
consuming it now would be
consuming poison
consuming it now would be slow
suicide
mind
we are going somewhere you can
explore your own power
we are going somewhere you'll
learn to trust what you decide
don't you hear me calling
haven't you heard
we're leaving this place behind
we're trying something renewed
mind
come back to me
haven't you heard
we're healing

unLYSHed

i line my mantle
with fruits from other places
my grandmother's garden
the market
galatians
i take a bite of them all
i let my pleasure escape from my
mouth
drip from my lips
and down my chin
i remember i had always loved fruit

then i decide to dance
the first song does not move me
but when i hear the violin strings
and falsettos
from track number 4
my body becomes a swan
a ballerina
fluent in movement
fluent in grace
i test new scents
new places
new books
i spread them out across my bed and
dive inside them
i measure my soul's response to be
gladness

i open my mouth
and let a song escape me
i sang like no one was listening
like the only One present was God
i remember
He loves my singing
i remember
how much i love to sing

when i finished i sat in the quiet
where there was no one to tell me
who to be
my LYSH raised her head
no one judged her
or crushed her
in the same room i had scaled walls
where i had ached for not being
liked
where i had grieved for having been
lost
i decided that i liked myself
i took time to find myself

sin
runs black
like tar
it smells of baking cobbler crust
bubbling with butter
i couldn't help myself
i tucked it under my tongue
i shot it into my bloodstream
i poured it into my mouth til it flooded my ears and my nose
i broke bread in hell for years
the evidence was in my eyes
in my hair
and wheelchair
and oxygen tank
sin was eating at my organs and my spirit man and still
i loved it
i wanted it
desire consumed me
what did i expect of my Father when i asked to be clean
the poison was to be sucked from my lips
the desire was to be stripped from my blood
God started my dialysis
then threw me into the meat grinder
i screamed every second
informing Him
it hurts
but didn't i ask for this
didn't i ask to be broken
what did i expect of my Father
how did i think He would make me well again
when i needed to be made
over
again

unLYSHed

lust is the nectar that drips from her lip
splinters decorate her fingers and her thighs
flesh is missing in the fruit next to her feet
this little girl
houses a woman in her body
a woman
fathered
by the tree of the knowledge of good and evil
the girl herself was born fallen
with desires too big for her small frame
with ability that does not match
the width of her mind
sinner
wretch
the earth would like to bed you
pump you full of pleasure
drive you into isolation
and leave you in the dark
beware of what they parade as freedom
beware of what happens in the dark
your woman tenant dips her hands into your soul
wraps it in wads around her palms
squeezes her fists
and pulls
the pride of the eye is your pride and joy
it holds you by your ankles
it keeps you from being
just a little girl
there is Blood to bathe your desires
blood that is bleach for what is wicked
blood that will allow you to finally
do as little girls do
when women are not housed in their bodies

you are my kind of indulgence
a guilty pleasure
chiseled by God's fingernails
skin
hair
hands
mouth
my fingers want you under my touch
i am your
temptation
my scent
turns you primal
you want to see what i'm made of
you want to know if it's sweet
you look at my legs as if they will be your gateway to glory
you could see God
if only you could get inside
so you mine the gold within my skin with your tongue
push your burdens into my belly
dip your fingers in the holy water my body makes for you
you see glory
you taste heaven
you are still broken
we climax to heaven's gates together
we come down to find
we've died a little
we seek the hovering Spirit
we stopped at each other
deep inside of me is not the deep you'll find Him
we've come here to come close
but my body was not broken for you
my body is breaking you
we cannot heal one another on this mattress stuffed with yonder's clouds
we cannot save one another by escaping in one another
when you leave this room
this bed
i will be more empty than when you found me
and you will look for another set of legs
that resemble
glory
another sacred dwelling
that you hope will bring you close to God

unLYSHed

the waters open up
they beg for my body
my fingers
my legs
my skin
my hair
they plea
to wash me over
to bury me beneath their fullness
to collapse over my flesh
they want me baptized
to shed my old body
to die to my obsessions
to sacrifice my trauma
to let rest my former self and all things that
trapped me
they want me to emerge
to be reintroduced to life
to scent
to touch
to sight
to sound
they want me to
taste and see
life as it is
God as He is
and that because of One
both are consistently
good
they want me to drip
in the happiness that is present
in this day
at this hour
to be refreshed
with healing currents
to be unLYSHed from the former
and to embrace
the now
the waters want for me to be free
in this way
we are the same

list of things i am releasing:
one
my grip
two
my secret plan
to turn my hands into crystal balls
three
my botched marriage to places that suffocate me
four
processed sugar after 9
five
judgment of avocado
six
the reins on my creativity
seven
laughter
seven
as loud and as often as it comes
eight
gratitude
eight
instead of grumbling
eight
for the withering
eight
and the budding
nine
the heartbreak and heartbreakers
ten
my breath
over
and over

unLYSHed

recipe for counteracting shame:

ingredients:
- ¼ cup of sugar
- 2 teaspoons of divulgence
- 2 cups of blackberries (fresh or frozen)
- a pinch of skin from the Cross
- 2 sticks of self-compassion
- 8 tablespoons of melted butter
- a small heap of empaths
- a heavy dose of psalm 139

directions:

mix all of the ingredients together.
consume them in one gulp.
let them bake into your heart and into your belly
let them change your mind
until you learn you can forgive yourself
until you come to accept yourself
until you love the way
your humanity tastes
until you realize
God loves the way
your humanity tastes

a whirlpool opens in my chest
it yawns and exposes its tongue
it covers my body
and turns me into the ocean
i am not underwater
i am the water
i am not in a storm
i am the storm
i regurgitate the skins i've worn with
the men
i'd swallowed
the ones that
rested under my bones
the hole that started in my chest
widens with greed
what will fill me
i ask
and manna from heaven
plugs my mouth
it settles my inconsolable existence
becomes tylenol for my heartache
becomes sustenance
that feeds my longing
it turns me into rippling water
i am no longer forceful enough to be waves
i am not the foam that makes it to the shore
i am not still nor am i raging
i am expanding
i am healing
and i am still worthy
i am still me

unLYSHed

i am making art of my thoughts
i am repurposing the evils
floating in my head

-       mental health awareness

i return to myself
i seek out the place where God was when i left Him
in the kitchen
the heart of the home
the heart in my body
i pop the top on time
we share servings in the safety of His presence
away from the noise
and the distractions
day by day
we grow closer

unLYSHed

list of things i am embracing:
one
the smell of the earth at 4am
two
every function of my body
three
the angels that stand by my bed while i sleep
four
my pen
four
what i can make with my pen
five
the wonder in my lips
five
in my fingers
five
in my hope
six
the girl inside the woman
seven
the beauty in not knowing
eight
the persistent time
nine
the yes and the amen that look like hope
nine
and a future
nine
and my mini me's
ten
the love i want to give to myself

on your knees
open your mouth

-       *it's time to confess*

unLYSHed

first
it is quiet
it is laying bare-bodied under the Son
and choosing not to move
until the damage in your skin starts to burn
until what is really unwell
shows itself to you
and then
it is confession
it is letting the pain speak
it is letting the wrong speak
it is sharing the depth
and the length
and what hurts
and how long
and then it is heavy
it is the blood that weighs 10,000 tons
it is what holds you in discomfort and in grief and in accountability
and then it is
forgiveness
it is baptism
and resurrection
and redemption
and protection
it is a shield from humiliation
and culpability
and then it is *love*
it is running Blood
and empty tomb
it is grandma's kisses
and it is hard bottom shoes
and then it is strength
it is how you are able to hold up your head again
to look in the mirror again
to say to yourself
i will love you and accept you and forgive you and encourage you and choose you
even when you fall

\-   *what is healing*

I remember the healing. How it came for my mind. How it didn't even find my mind in my head. How my mind had left home. How it had been consuming foolishness. And swine slop. How my mind had to be extracted from hyena bellies and incisors. How it had been amidst the chaotic. Amidst the reckless. How it found itself swallowed whole. How healing saw it all as it turned my mind around in its palms. How healing found things upside down. And shattered. And hiding. Behind picture frames. Behind faces. How perception had been hammered. How my sight and my feeling were both impaired. How enabling was posing as love. How residue from old LYSH was in dust. In dirt. On windowsills and blades of ceiling fans. How healing found evils in the shadows. Consuming the light with resentment. With sickness. With lovelessness. With idols. How healing showed me my sin. How healing showed me Whose Heart I broke. How healing showed me the hearts I broke. How guilt went savage as I began to see. How it salivated and attacked and tried to consume me. Tried to consume my mind. How my surrender had put the healing in charge. How healing made guilt to heel. How healing tracked my thoughts and caught self-hate and self-harm by the necks. How it put shame on a leash. How it dipped my mind in The Blood, and it screamed. How it dipped my mind in The Blood, and I screamed. How my body contorted. How healing burned out the evils. How healing arrested my wayward thoughts and made them kneel. In The Blood. How healing brought in accountability with forgiveness. How healing brought in humanity and respect. How they all wore red. How I knew I had always liked red. How my mind began to look more like a safe space. How healing gave it back to me as sound. With everything in its place.

With new tricks learned. With a supply of The Blood for a daily cleanse. How my mind was made clean. I remember the healing. Healing came for my mind and gave my mind **rest**.

I remember the healing. How it came for my body. How it undressed me. How it took me in. From the strands of my hair. To the swelling of my belly. To the soles of my feet. How it prepared to stay a while. I felt healing touch me. I felt healing begin its work. As it cut healthy skin and stretched it over the skin that was burned. As it reset my backbones and rib cages. As it entered and exited my flesh to stitch the gashes. As it crawled down my throat to regrow my fingers and forearms. As it carried me to the bath to wash away my blood. With The Blood. The Blood consumed me, and my body screamed. The Blood consumed me, and my body writhed. The Blood consumed me, and my body ached. How I clutched healing's hem as the pain rippled through me. As the bad habits darkened the bloodwater. As the self-hate and self-harm ran out of my pores. As the insults I held in my skin evaporated. As the souls I housed inside my body slipped out from between my legs. As The Blood covered it all. As The Blood helped my body forgive it all. As my body returned from those who broke it. As it came back to the one charged to steward it. As it settled back into itself. As it became familiar with rightness. As it practiced its function. As it began to work in tandem with the mind. The mind that had already experienced The Blood. How I didn't let my body up. Not until my body had been soaked in The Blood. Not until my body laughed. And stretched. And bent. And danced. And bloomed. And rested. I remember the healing. The healing came for my body and gave my body **rest**.

I remember the healing. How it came for my spirit. How it showed me what couldn't be solved in the mind nor in the body. How it went back to the idols. And the swollen belly. How it pumped my spirit until golden chunks came out of my eyes. How it pumped my spirit until golden chunks came out of my mouth. How the pieces assembled themselves before me and revealed to me their bodies. How the pieces assembled themselves before me and revealed to me their names. Approval. Control. Self-Sufficiency. How healing pumped up 20 years' worth of idolatry undigested. How healing pumped up an influence that I hadn't seen. Like how Fear gave the orders and Approval obliged. Approval whispered. Approval told me to mask. It shamed me when I was rejected. It taught me I didn't deserve a love. A space. A chance. Or grace. How it was responsible for how I lost my LYSH. How it mocked me and abandoned me and hid behind Fear. How it was insufficient as a god. How it had not loved me but had failed me. Healing showed me Control. How Fear gave the orders and Control obliged. How Control was the cause of the panic attacks. The broken dishes. The misplaced faith. How it encouraged me to control what i never could. Like people's actions. Like people's feelings. Like people's lives. And how long they kept them. And when they lost them. Like God's thoughts. Like God's plans. And it disgraced me. For failing. How that led me to numb. How that taught me to punish LYSH. How that helped me to distract by what I could control. How it taught me to chase. And to take small spaces. How it mocked me and abandoned me and hid behind Fear. How it was insufficient as a god.

How it had not loved me but had failed me. Healing showed me Self-Sufficiency. How Fear gave the orders and Self-Sufficiency obliged. How Self-Sufficiency was the one who helped break perception. How it taught me to depend solely on myself. How it favored isolation. How I obeyed. And I tried. And the more I thought I did to bail me out the heavier my chains became. How when The Voices started, I told no one. How when the strangers came, I told no one. How I became more lost with every act I performed. How Self-Sufficiency ruled in my impatience. How it ruled in my ignorance. How it led me to save myself then humiliated me. For not having saving power. How it mocked me and abandoned me and hid behind Fear. How it was insufficient as a god. How it had not loved me but had failed me. I remember the healing. Healing showed me **how fear had birthed them all.**

I remember the healing.
It came in community. In the church folk. In the sisterhood.
In the family with the same blood. In the family without the same blood.
I remember the healing.
It came in time. It took pruning. And mirrors. And confession. And surrender. And choosing not to get up from the table. And choosing not to get out of the tub.
I remember the healing.
It came in releasing. The bad words. The bad moments. The bad blood. The wrong idea.
I remember the healing.
It came in trial.
In discerning. And in doxology. And letting it all flow through.
I remember the healing.

It came in exhaling.
In psalms. In poems. In praise.
I remember the healing.
It came in the cold.
And in the valley.
And in the fire.
And through The Word.
And in The Blood.
And under the Son.
And by the Son.

i am awake now
God has given me a third eye
i see people and i see
the pandemic within the pandemic
i have not been the only one hiding
people are in closets
in costume
in insecurity
in liquor bottles
i have not been the only one bleeding
blood is seeping through her sleeve
blood is running from their skulls
i have not been the only one masking
wearing skins
and smiles
each tells its own lie
they throw passersby off of trauma's scent
some are so numb
they can no longer hear their spirit groaning
some are so numb
they no longer remember to remove the mask
those who waited too late to start the healing
feel no guilt
no responsibility
no sorrow
or anything at all
when you look at you
do you see you
when you look at you do you think you've hurt enough

- *the necessity of healing*

happy

God made me a new creature
and put me back in my mother's arms

- *happy is at home*

my soul is freshly exfoliated
she is giving off a remarkable glow

unLYSHed

the warm, heavy cream
vanilla
and chai
that avalanche down my mountain tongue
and blanket my taste buds in sweetness
the glinting treasure of a broach of moonlight that adorns
the midnight that cloaks me
the comfort that marches into my heart to the rhythmic purr of my mother's pulse
the current of electricity that flows through my hope that is casket sharp
the heavy-handed God Who pours out His spirit
Who pools and overflows as the Oasis in my desert soul
for this
my straightjacket of bed unbuckles my body
for this
my belly that for days has not opened its mouth
grumbles to ask for a taste of something filling
for this
my eyes let in the light
for this
song floods my throat and spills into my home
for this
i give the day
a chance

-     *the practice of gratitude*

i was born in a bathroom
i crawled out of the corpse that was set on fire
in a bathtub full of gasoline
the ashes left from the burning
are the same that shaped my head
flame became friend
i stood
tile and ruin beneath my feet
i shuffled my feathers and stroked the skin across my chest
a woman
a phoenix
born in a bathroom
born from flame
i belong in the ether
with the dragons
and other flying things
where there is room for my wingspan
where no one wishes to force me into chains
museums
or boxes
or bathrooms
where there is space for my legs
and my neck cannot become cramped
i am the phoenix
born in a bathroom
who flies with dragons
who sits under the nose of God

- *beauty for ashes*

unLYSHed

what if
before we are anything to anyone else
we are everything we can be
to ourselves

you come from a long line of the
saccharine
with legs the length of 200 caramel
chews
your back smooth like whipped
honey butter
your face and hands and thighs
dotted with chocolate chip freckles
your belly
a tender gummy bear
your hair
cotton candy puffs
your lips, studded and stained with
candy apple syrup
you are made up of things made
mistakes
burn marks
dust and sugar cane
you make up what was not made for
you
the path
the space
the love
look how you stretch
like taffy
your beauty touches every corner of
every room
you deserve to be tasted
to be savored
to be cherished as a rarity
a sweet tooth's dream
a candy land vision something only
seen in fairy-tales
but you should be hugged like
you're real
tightly to the chest as by a 2-year-
old holding a candy treasure
you should be cradled
gently
as if you were as fragile as a candy
cane

you should be craved
heart melter
you should be earned
heart helper
you deserve to be
preserved
to live and to do and to remain
the embodiment of sweetness
covered in candy wrappers and
protection prayers
i honor you
with well treatment
and with favoritism
i am a fan of you

-       *ode to my body*

unLYSHed

today i tried
i found myself at couldn't
i couldn't be beautiful
i couldn't be creative
i was committed to misery
i wore it like a scratchy coat
i was committed to inability
i grated it against my face
i was committed to intimidation
i dove into a glass full
i swiped my desk clean of its monitors and its picture frames
i drove them straight into a cemented wall
and then i followed them
ran head-first into the stone
i thought maybe i'd shatter too
i didn't
i brought my hand to my aching head
and lay against the floor as laughter shook my body, thinking
i could try to get to *could* tomorrow
or maybe
in an hour

-    *healing exists in happy*

one
vanilla ice cream is better with oreo chunks
two
family is synonymous to *fortress*
three
the grinch is my alter ego
four
when defending those i love
no beast would cross me
five
my softness is under lock and key until it is safe for her to surface
five
sometimes she steals glances
five
she finds the time is not quite right
six
for me it has been better to dream than to see
seven
love is my love language
eight
i like it in every tongue
eight
in every way that it comes
nine
i have an audacity
nine
it keeps me in places i wasn't invited
nine
the same places i've always belonged
nine
the same places i make
mine
ten
in every strand of my hair
in the grooves of my fingerprints
in the arches of my feet
i long
for God

\-   *still discovering my sunflower petals*

unLYSHed

last night i visited the love i was forced to let go
there is a place
where we meet
it is only accessed in my dreams
as i walked the grounds
i saw *your* love
smelling the clouds
swimming butterfly strokes in the sun's rays
i could only stay
for as long as i could sleep
but happy does not seem strong enough to fit the vision that shaped inside my head
both your love
and mine
were
whole

-       *for the grieving*

when i think of you
my imagination turns into a writing desk
hope
takes up the pen
hope
begins to describe wonder
have you ever considered how eternity might dress
if it has to prepare for winter
or if it lays out on beaches and sands
have you ever wondered what God is like
how much of Him is much too much to consider
i don't know what ultimate wholeness does to desire
i don't think God is boring
i do think eternity is a long time
and i do think that glory is full of surprises
things our human minds could never fathom
wonders that we have never beheld
i believe that if nothing else
when you get there
you'll have Someone to love

- *for the childless who didn't want to be childless*

unLYSHed

forward is faceless
she cannot be seen until she becomes
present
now
then forward
is reborn
forward takes on a new face
she is impossible to catch
but worthy of the chase
in every place she leaves
there is freshness
vibrance
challenge
and the opportunity to go
forward
over again

free:

Captivity came to claim me.
It was years after "break me." After wrath. After healing.
And when it came, it came in purpose. With authority. With a voice that made my skin prickle. It came with the idols. The Voices. And The Only Man I Ever Wanted to Call "*Baby.*"
Naturally, Fear produced himself.
Naturally, Fear put his hands on me.
The voice of Captivity spoke. It reminded me of my old paths. Old ways. Old love. Old gods. Old skin. Old cage. Old chains. As he spoke, he threatened me. With images. With film. Of the consequences of *denying him.* Of not taking *what I deserved.* Of a life where no one else would see me. No one else would want me. And *there was nothing I could do to save myself.*
Captivity told me to come.
Captivity told me to come, and I felt my feet move.
I remembered old LYSH and how she lost her tongue in The Sunflower Project. How she lost her LYSH to narcissism. How she didn't scream and didn't fight. The LYSH who believed she was without choices and permission. The LYSH whose voice was stolen by trauma. The LYSH who sat at her kitchen table and wrote out her fears knowing that where she feared was where she trusted God the least. The LYSH who prayed the break me prayer—
The LYSH who had already been broken.
And **I** *had already seen God.*
The way Ezekiel did. When God stretched out His hand and pulled him up into His spirit. When God commanded Ezekiel to command the bones. When God commanded Ezekiel to command the breath. When together they made a dead, and dry thing, rise. *He came to me.* God. The way He did Ezekiel. Just when I had begun to feel changed. After the blood that held the heaviness had been filtered out. When body, mind, soul, and spirit were all like newborn babies, tasting life for the first time, stretching beyond the barriers of usual confinements, giving "healthy" their best attempts. When dates, moments, and offenses I had clung to and lived in the shadow of, were fading. Less terrifying. Less emotion-evoking. When I had died to thinking that I didn't deserve good things. When I had died to

unLYSHed

believing that God was good, but shouldn't want to be good to me. When I was relearning how to walk, and I slipped and hit hopelessness, *but responded like I was new*. When I did not shame. When I did not mask. When I did not revert. But took time to confess. I stopped and surrendered. I told God about The Voices. And the urges. To harm. To hurt. To quit. And I asked God to *do* something. And God got involved. He sent His Spirit into my room, and He filled it with wind. He stretched out His hand and pulled me up from my bed. He drew me into His arms. He swaddled my body with my sheets. He nestled me into His chest.

He rocked me back to sleep.
When I awakened, I was still just shy of happy.
I still had desire.
Still thirsted.
Still waited.
Things were still a little dead.
Things were still a little dry.

But Dangerous Prayers had seized my trust issues so faith in God could *consume* me. So I would know what to do when Captivity came. And I knew what to do when Captivity came. *I called on the Son.* Who appeared before me. Who saw my feet moving. Whom I asked to decide for me.

Who, in that moment, *refused to decide for me*.

He would not *take* my will. He would not take my decision. He did not stop my feet, and immediately I felt like Eve. Like I was in the middle of Eden between two trees. Two choices. In the wake of her capacity to pick wrongly—and then I felt like *LYSH*. In the time before the healing. Where I had lived for 7 months. And 10 years. And 3 weeks. And maybe even a lifetime. A LYSH who had not trusted herself.

A LYSH who had been consumed by Fear.

A LYSH who had been dismantled.

A LYSH who thought she had no right to her no, or to the yes and the amen, but who had been in the middle. Between becoming and being. Between bitter and sweet. Between darkness and goodness. Between bondage and freedom. I was looking at the Son, seconds away from being thrust back into Captivity and He was telling me to open my mouth. To use my tongue. To decide. To reclaim. To choose my own path. *To say what I wanted.*

Me.

Then it all made sense.

When I surrendered my life, my wants, and my all, to Jesus, just before my break me season, I had done so because I was tired of not working right. Of choosing wrong. Of not knowing what it meant to *live*. Of believing enough to be saved, but not believing enough to be consumed by God.

When I confessed my fears, He had hidden me. For 7 months. And 3 weeks. And 3 more years post 10.

When I asked to be broken, I was still in surrender. I had not been able to choose how the breaking happened. Or how healing came. Or how long it took. I had given up my autonomy. I had given up my choice. And here in the face of what had been my familiar, as The Only Man I Ever Wanted to Call "*Baby*," let "I love you," drip from his lips, and stood before me as the potential resolve to my fears, the man I had adored, my relationship with him the symbol for me of a life *committed* to Fear—*the Son had told me to* **choose**.

So, I paused. And thought. If maybe there was another dimension of revelation within Dangerous Prayers that I had not considered. God wanted to give me the desires of my heart, but I hadn't even *known* them outside of Fear. I hadn't prayed for them without a tainted heart of desperation. I hadn't allowed myself to want them since they had been dipped in The Blood. So I named my desires in contrast to my fears, and said them aloud.

Three: I didn't want to be successful *just* to avoid poverty or to prove to those who rejected me that I was worthy of their acceptance; or to prove to myself that I was worthy of anything. I wanted to live a life in purpose and in alignment with God's will. I wanted to know that no matter how the seasons changed He alone made me worthy... of everything.

Two: I didn't want to *just* be a mother; I wanted to be made safe and stable enough *to* mother; to love, to lead, and to teach in a way that honors God–humble enough to let Him love *through* me in the lives that will grow inside me and in the lives of His children I'm called to touch.

One: I didn't *just* want to have someone filling a space for a partner, a husband, a lover, a father. I wanted to have the future God selected for me; the Forever that God already wrote for me. I wanted to have love that reached all my dry spots, and to give love that was not too heavy or that returned. *I* wanted a Safe Place to Land and to *be* a Safe Place to Land.

unLYSHed

Break me, the wrath, the woe, and the healing were so that *I* could trust God, yet through the entire journey–*He* had trusted *me*. To return to Him. To take His yoke upon me. To survive the flames. And in and out of season, and in and out of battle to *choose Him*. The Father broke me to stop me from fearing the fears. And the lonely. And the unknown. And the yet to be seen. He broke me to bring back the sweetness. To clear my vision. To learn to forgive. Who hurt me. And myself for who I'd hurt. And myself for the LYSH I'd hurt. He broke me and my heart ailed. For how I had made Him grieve. For how long He had gone without all of my love. For how long He had longed for me. And yet, here He was–my sins and my shortcomings in Captivity's report, echoing all over this Eden, damning me to emptiness and scarcity and destitution and *God* Himself, was offering me a choice. Like what I had done didn't matter. Like what had been done to *me*, didn't matter. Like He didn't remember the offenses against Him at all. Like He didn't remember that I gave up my choice because I couldn't be trusted to choose. He was empowering me to try again. He was restoring my authority, and even while I flirted with Fear, He hadn't left me. He was still willing to let me have Captivity without losing *Him*. I could have an existence based on the knowledge of good and evil—or a taste of a *life* with His Son as *my* life.

    In that moment, I recognized grace.
    In that moment, I recognized mercy.
    In that moment, I recognized *Love*.
    The truest desire of my heart.
    Even when I was a little girl.
    I wanted to be everything I was and everything I carried and not be turned away; I wanted Love unconditionally. I wanted Love everlastingly. And I finally saw Him before me, wanting to be chosen, still waiting for *me*—after 7 months, 10 years, 3 weeks and a lifetime. He had loved me. He still loved me.
    And I wanted *Him*.
    I chose Him.
    I spoke directly to Fear in the tongue of the second Timothy.
    I freed the one who was once the only man I ever wanted to call baby from the possibility of being miserably together.
    And then I turned to Christ.
    The One Who had come for me.

Who had pursued me. Who had trusted me. Who empowered me to choose, to fail, to get up, to live on. Who reminded me I could be broken, flawed, bruised and cut and not lose His love.

I took steps toward Him on the fragments of the golden calves, their altars, and my old chains, as white satin draped and embellished my frame. I kept my eyes locked onto His as I made it to the altar, the train of my gown blowing behind me in the wind. Beyond Him, sunflowers rose from the earth. The angels descended from heaven. And seated next to one another was the family of the bride. All of the souls of those who had loved me, defended me, stood with me and prayed for me.

As I reached Him, I gave Him my hands.

He held them in His own.

And the holes didn't bother me a bit.

I repledged my loyalty, commitment, and fidelity to *Him*—my Forever Love. My God, my Savior, and My Comforter all in one, and sealed our covenant with, "*I always will*," before my head rested against His chest, and then—at 28 years old—I prepared to live. For the first time.

***

I believed I was already saved, but something was different. From my little girl faith. From my flimsy faith. I had seen miracles. *I had seen Love*. I had seen a God Who was truly worthy of my fear. One Who could weave in and out of time and cause a disruption that split my life at its head and turned it on itself. One Who was close enough to hear my faintest whispers. My private confessions. My secret poems. My darkest fears. One Whose power was both terrifying and liberating. One known as the God Who sees. The One Who sought and found that my soul could love Him. The One Who had always loved me. The One Who broke me to teach me to trust. The one Who broke me to give me *freedom*.

> **freedom:**
> *fear's reckoning. faith's mother. God's gift. it's in exhales. in unclenched fists. in closed eyes. in selah. it's learning to breathe through the contractions. without tensing. without fighting. it's giving up your will and your body and your life. to the One Who keeps you from falling. to the One Who doesn't*

think you're "too." it's crawling into Him to receive the only Truth. that in Him you cannot lose. in Him you cannot die. that in Him you cannot be burned, even if the earth is on fire. even if the earth is consumed. it's backstroking in the pool of God's eye to receive **an enlightened mind. an enraptured spirit. an enlarged heart.**

***

I rotate my head in the crooks of my shoulders and settle in from my new perspective.

Since I've grown wings, I see life from a different view.

Sonlight feels warmer.

The oxygen tastes like pomegranate.

And mercy.

I guzzle it down with every inhale.

I'm still getting used to my body—my feathers. I feel my flesh stretching into position underneath my skin. The soles of my feet become lighter, my hands reach and hold tenderly, my tongue practices saying what *is*, and I feel a sense of *relief*. I am soaring over **happy**. It's at the corner of blind and belief. Just north of deep breath. Next to the extended definition of beauty. And of strength. The ones that encompass the grieving. The childless. The abused. The victims. The survivors. The healers. The humans. Where the housing is built upon Truth. Where disappointment sometimes visits with contentment. Where peace and desire arm wrestle on coffee tables. Where there is *love*. Where there is *safety*. Where life is welcome, and it does not consume me. I find myself in *happy*. Consumed with the One Who changed my portion. The One Who changed my name. The One Who makes me **free**.

she is a cave at the base of Calvary's hill
her hair is made of overgrown grass
rubble
peonies
and blood stains
i stroke it as i walk inside
creatures chase one another in the hollow of her mouth
they are named
one is desire
the other is fulfillment
the earth speaks to me as i take step
i lift my left and earth giggles
i lift my right and earth groans
just past the paths for purpose and pride
i hear rushing water
the water is blue
yet the water is named
content
memory falls from the ceiling and fills her throat
grief rides the rush like an otter on its back
birds blow into the space
their wings feathered with possibility and timidity
happy is so frightening
happy is so beautiful
the sight sends me into overwhelm
i launch myself into the pool and she swallows me whole
deep inside her belly
as the tears fall
and chill bumps rush across my skin
i float amongst all of the things that live inside
of happy

-       *she is found*

for years
the window was not open
i drove nails into its base
bonded it to the sill
painted the glass with smuts and tar
i covered the ground beneath it with poisoned seed
to keep the birds
and their song
away
i banned the sunlight
i called myself mourning
i couldn't
let the laughter in
and then You
turned me tender
You soaked me in regeneration marinade
and baked me slowly
to collapse never felt so good as it did before You
plated with surrender
and with value
You want to consume me
to squeeze me with more than happy
to turn my existence into a Godwink
i accept
i receive Your offering
i accept You as my life

- *dear God*

now that you've read:

this book was inspired by a real-life experience of seeing a Real-Life God respond to my Dangerous Prayers, a bible plan and book authored by Craig Groeschel, which i completed in the midst of the pandemic. within 45 days of praying the break me prayer, i realized that my fears had come to consume me—but God had another plan for my life. i want to give a special thank you to Craig Groeschel and other spiritual leaders whose ministry aided me through my "break me" season. The Holy Spirit guided me to each of you in specific windows for understanding and Truth, and I honor you for your obedience to your call:

My Pastor, Dr. Carl Wardlaw, Jr.
Dr. Carl Anthony Wardlaw
Carl Wardlaw, III
Jackie Hill Perry
Dr. Charles Goodman of Tabernacle Baptist Church
Lysa Terkeurst, Author of Forgiving What You Can't Forget

additionally, i say thank you to chandler moore, and all of maverick city music - also to daily grace co (creators of the idolatry study)— your ministries ripped me open and threw me into surrender. you are appreciated.

acknowledgements:

i thank God for not leaving me to die in sin or in misery, but for receiving me unto Himself. Father, i give you my "always." always.

to the eMpire—i thought of who you are and who you've been to define "happy." i found that happy can exist among chaos because happy is where i am loved and where i am safe. you were and have been exactly that—thank you for being my home. mommy, daddy, cRew, sister, and baby DRU—thank you for making up my "happy."

shoota—thank you for sticking with me, and letting me lean on you as i completed this work and lived through this season. thank you for staying for the good parts and the roughest parts. For being the first person to hear my poetry and the first to read my stories in the unLYSHed way. for always having time, never finding me too heavy, keeping your finger on the trigger, and my name in God's ear. love. protect. defend. respect. 4life.

my lea and rudolphdurant—thank you for loving me through all my stages, and for being my family. thank you for not minding my highs or lows, and never growing tired of being by my side. 4ever.

Ri, Tip, Zoe, Shelbi—thank you for being the community that held the mirror for me. your insight, your prayers, and your love created for me a home away from home, and i thank you for barricading me with light and companionship. i love you.

macey—wow. thank you for being my whole unofficial therapist, friend, spiritual counsel and sister. thank you for guiding me through the scriptures, praying for me daily, and believing in this birth. your sacrifice was monumental for my healing, and i thank you. your love reached me no matter how far away i wandered, and i thank you.

uncle tony—thank you for catching me when my heartbreak sent me reeling. for introducing me to psalm 91. for being my sounding board, my wise counsel, and my wake-up call. thank you for reminding me of who God called me to be, and of my responsibility to the kingdom just as well as to myself. thank you for always giving me Jesus and an overflow of an uncle's love.

to my grandma, who is really my second mama—thank you for fixing me breakfast every morning of my recovery & making me eat like a champion when i was still trying to feel like one. thank you for being a mother, guide, nurturer, and comfort all the years of my life. i love you.

to my mccloud and wardlaw family—thank you for loving me—for visiting me on my sick bed, for bringing cards and gifts and flowers to keep me encouraged and (auntie freda) for keeping me regal on recovery with my special loungewear sets. my whole life you have made special. i think your existence makes

unLYSHed

*me special. i will ever guard you and love you with all i have, and i thank God always for you.

    chelsi—my big sister and my big queen—thank you for pouring into me with Godly wisdom; for giving me relationship and mentorship; for supporting my visions and my brand; for literally helping me to take brave steps toward my unLYSHed self without letting go of my hand. you have seen me and stood with me and i love you.

    jared and jackson—for the entirety of this experience, your love for me gave me the grace to crumble and the power to stand, day in and day out. thank you for seeing me, for accepting all of me, and for keeping my little blue chair ready for my visits. you are so loved.

    queen li—thank you for trusting me and my special gifts; thank you for the sacrifice of your time, your wisdom, and your friendship. thank you for giving me a space to speak and become familiar with my own voice; thank you for always encouraging me to be myself when i wasn't sure i could trust myself. i love you.

    God's daughters and my special friends that God appointed to pour at a designated time—your obedience provided me nourishment and exhortation, and funneled into me His power. **mikaelafunndip, jasmine tyrone, and taymunson**, i thank you. i love you.

    phoenix—thank you for pointing me in the direction of increase. your insight and special gifts helped me become a greater version of LYSH and i am grateful.

    to my cousin-hype-team and my own special reasons—**thebadgirlsclub, jessikay, and ooh**—thank you for existing. your life alone helped me to be brave. to keep fighting. so that God's work on me and through me may make me a little more worthy of being your big sister. love you.

    to auntie angie—i love and miss you. i wish you could've seen this part.

    andddd to my entire family, all my sisterfriends, my mother figures, my hometown, clark atlanta, and to *you*, whoever you are, holding this baby in your hands—i thank you for journeying with me. for teaching me. for stretching me. for loving me down. for opening your heart up to receive the Spirit of God weaved throughout these pages—and for making space for all of me.

    all my love—until next time.

LYSH

about the author:
alyssia charisse mccloud, who writes as unLYSHed, welcomed writing as a part of her identity in 2017 as a senior at Clark Atlanta University. While serving as Miss CAU, LYSH hosted an event where she was able to perform her poetry publicly for the first time, openly speaking of her battle with mental health after the shatter experienced as a survivor of relational trauma. God breathed a freshness into LYSH's life and healing during this season – one that came from His mercy and the writing and sharing of her story. *The Sunflower Project* and *Consumed: The Survivor's Story*, are two self-published products birthed from LYSH's soul; they tell of how a girl came to be a woman; how a woman who thought she had to settle as anybody's, became somebody in Christ; and of how "somebody" became unLYSHed - worthy, loved, healed, freed - when she gave God her "yes." As unLYSHed, LYSH developed the PetalxStrokes platform where she blends her professional identity as a becoming mental health counselor with her passion and gift as a poet, writer, and artist, through which she inspires other trauma survivors to write through their stories and to grow *from fragmented to found*. LYSH's hope is that through her continued witness as a narcissistic abuse and sexual assault survivor and a Daughter of the King, that those who have the same scars as her, will choose to heal and to know their *unlyshed* selves by running to the Creator - for love that is true and never fails; for a healed self-image; for an existence approaching wholeness; and for a much-deserved *rest*.

The PetalxStrokes platform can be found on YouTube and Instagram at the handle: @petalxstrokes.

unLYSHed

CONSUMED: THE SURVIVOR'S STORY

unLYSHed

Made in the USA
Middletown, DE
17 January 2025

68810223R00076